# DISCOVER THE **MOST AMAZING BIKES** ON EARTH!

# MEGA BOOK OF
# MOTORCYCLES

ALLIGATOR
www.alligatorbooks.co.uk

# CONTENTS

# BIKE BASICS

From nipping down to the shops to touring the countryside or speeding on a racing circuit, there are different motorcycles for every kind of driver. On the following pages you'll find bikes ranging from the earliest wooden and brass models, to the most powerful designs of today. Take a look at some of the wacky 'oddballs' that have appeared over the years – or drool over the most expensive motorcycles imaginable! First, let's look at the basics.

*Storage compartment*

*The four main sections of a motorcycle are: the frame, the engine (with gearbox and drive components), the wheels and the petrol tank.*

*Passenger back rest*

*Motorcycles (like this Harley-Davidson tourer) have wire-spoked wheels, whereas scooters usually have solid wheels like those of a car.*

*Exhaust*

## MEGA MILEAGE

*Depending on the size of the engine, a motorcycle may run up to 36 km per litre (85 miles per gallon) — about four times that of most mid-sized cars.*

## SAFETY FIRST

There's no doubt about it — motorcycles can be dangerous if they're not used correctly. Training is a must: steering, accelerating and braking require skill and a high degree of co-ordination. The proper outfit is essential too. In addition to the helmet (which is vital) motorcyclists need to wear as much leather clothing as possible to protect them should they fall. This includes gloves, boots, jackets and chaps or full-body riding suits.

*The term 'cc' refers to the cylinder capacity of a vehicle. The bigger the cc — the more power you get! Cylinder capacity of a motorcycle can range from 250 to 1,500 or even higher.*

*The front wheel and axle are attached to the frame with a 'fork', a two-pronged pivoting arm.*

*Disc brake*

*Handlebar control for the engine*

*Petrol tank*

*Two-stroke and four-stroke engines are used for motorcycles. The power is transmitted to the rear wheel through the gearbox and then through sprockets and chains, or through a drive shaft.*

# BONESHAKERS

Motorcycles have been around for over 100 years but it's difficult to recognise the very first models as the same sleek, powerful machines we know today. They originally descended from push bikes, and most of the first motorcycles were little more than ordinary bicycles with a simple motor attached which drove the back wheel. Some of these 'boneshakers' even had pedals – so the rider could help the motor!

**MEGA FACT**
*The first motorised bicycle, the Michaux-Perraux, was built in 1868. It reached a maximum speed of 30 km/h (19 mph) on its first short run.*

**A BUMPY RIDE**
Early models were called 'boneshakers' for good reason. Their lack of suspension, plus the bumpy country roads of the day, meant cyclists were in for a shaky ride!

# THE FIRST MOTORCYCLE

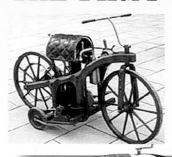

It was German engineer Gottlieb Daimler (who later formed the Daimler-Benz company with Karl Benz) who earned the nickname 'Father of the Motorcycle'.

In 1885, Daimler built the first motorcycle that used petrol. It was constructed mostly of wood, with wooden-spoked, iron-banded wagon wheels. But the vehicle also had two smaller wheels at either side, and technically this disqualified it as a true bicycle. Yet most historians consider this model to be the first motorcycle. Daimler's son, Paul, was the first to ride his father's invention, for nearly 10 km (6 miles) – until the engine became so hot it set the saddle on fire!

## PART EXCHANGE

Regular bicycle wheels soon became too weak for motorcycles, and sturdier designs were constructed to take their place. Pedals disappeared altogether as more powerful engines came on the market.

## A PLACE IN HISTORY

The motorcycle was the world's first form of personal mechanised transport, pre-dating the car by 25 years. Designers of early motorcycles took a long time deciding where to put the engine. One memorable model even towed its engine in a trailer!

**MEGA FACT**
*In 1881, a steam tricycle was exhibited at the Stanley Bicycle Show in London. Despite attracting many orders, British law made it illegal for such self-powered vehicles to be used on public roads at the time!*

BONESHAKERS

# THOMAS AUTO-BI

In 1900, American E.R. Thomas designed the Auto-Bi motorcycle, shown below (although it's little more than a bicycle with a motor attached!). In 1905, W.C. Cadeayne caused quite a stir when he established a new record by riding his Auto-Bi across the country in just 48 days!

**MEGA FACT**
*The Thomas Auto-Bi was the USA's first mass-produced motorcycle.*

# IVER JOHNSON

Made by Iver Johnson's Arms and Cycle Works in Massachussetts, USA, this top-of-the-range 1915 model was said to 'ride like a touring car'. Unusually, the top and middle frame tubes bend over the engine.

**MEGA FACT**
*The inflatable tyre, which gave a much smoother ride than the old wagon wheels, was invented in 1888, by John Boyd Dunlop.*

# CLEVELAND A2

By 1918, cars were becoming widely available, putting motorcycle makers under great pressure; if they could afford it, many people preferred a car. But while a Model T Ford would have cost US$625 (with extras) in 1919, the A2 only cost US$150 – good value for a reliable motorcycle. The 1918 A2 became one of the most popular motorcycles of the time not only because of its low cost – it didn't weigh much (making it easy to ride and park), and the engine was easy to maintain.

**MEGA FACT**
*In 1912, Carl Stevens Clancy was the first motorcyclist to travel around the world. Starting in the USA, he went through Europe, Africa, Japan and finished in New York – a distance of some 29,000 km (18,000 miles).*

# INDIAN DAYTONA TWIN

The 1920 Indian Daytona Twin was one of the sleekest, fastest racing motorcycles of its day, when races were held on simple dirt-track courses. Although this bike's top speed was 170 km/h (106 mph), its brakes and suspension were poor – so a rider's mistakes could easily end in an accident.

**MEGA FACT**
*In 1914, the manufacturer Indian produced the first motorcycle with an electric starter.*

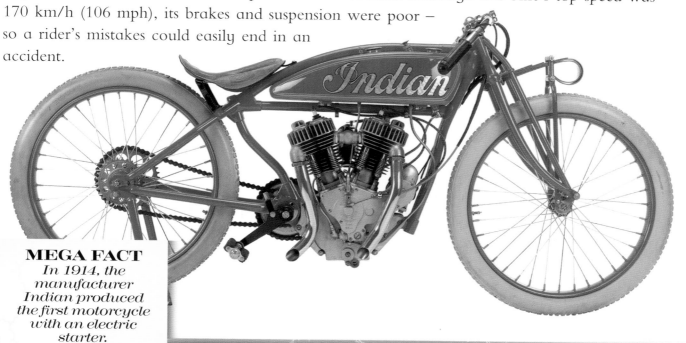

# THE CLASSICS

For almost a century now, the name Harley-Davidson has been synonymous with motorcycles. Since the company began production with the 'Silent Gray Fellow' in 1904, Harley-Davidson has never looked back. But other manufacturers of the day, such as Triumph, Indian and Honda, have given us a few well-loved classics to remember too...

### ALL-TIME CLASSIC

When it comes to motorcycles, the 1936 Harley-Davidson 61E wins the vote for the classic of all-time! A highly technical model, it set the design for all Harleys that followed. With its rounded tank, stylish instrument console and curving mudguards, the 61E quickly took the lead in American motorcycle design.

### PUSH-ME-PULL-YOU

The front and back wheels of the Harley-Davidson 61E were interchangeable, which was a common feature of motorcycles during the 1930s.

*Big Harleys are nicknamed 'Hogs' because of their great size.*

### MEGA CLASSIC
*When Harley-Davidson was first incorporated in 1907, the company made only 150 motorcycles in a year. By 1909, production had increased to eight times that amount.*

# HARLEY-DAVIDSON MILESTONES

**1901** Harley-Davidson founders begin design experiments

**1907** The Harley-Davidson company is incorporated

**1909** Trademark 45 degree V-Twin engine is introduced

**1916–18** Harleys called to duty in World War I

**1920** H-D becomes the world's largest motorcycle manufacturer

**1936** The H-D Knucklehead is introduced

**1939–44** Harleys called to duty in World War II

**1965** Land speed record is set on a modified Harley Sprint

**1976-8** Harleys win the AMA Championship three years running

## THE 'KNUCKLEHEAD'

The 61E earned this name as the engine resembled a clenched fist. The rocker covers form the 'knuckles'!

## EASY RIDERS

Not all motorcyclists like riding super fast – many like to sit back and cruise along the open road. These bikers are called 'Easy Riders'. To them, style and comfort are more important than speed. Harleys are the world's most popular bikes with Easy Riders.

## MEGA DUTY
*In 1907, Harley-Davidsons were being sold for police duty for the first time. Harleys were also used later by the military in both World Wars.*

# BMW R1200 C

In one of the most dramatic chase scenes ever seen on film, James Bond skilfully rides a BMW R1200 over the rooftops in the 1997 movie, *Tomorrow Never Dies*. It was one of very few motorcycles ever to be used in a James Bond film, and it's not difficult to see why the movie-makers chose this particular model. The R1200 was BMW's first ever cruiser, launched in 1997, but with its high US-style handlebars and impressive five-speed gearbox, it's already becoming a truly modern classic.

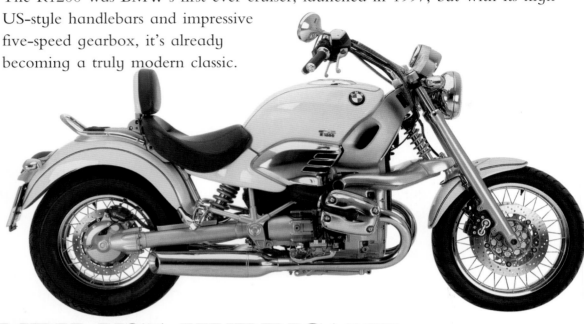

# TRIUMPH X75 HURRICANE

Britain's Craig Vetter was commissioned by BSA-Triumph to style a limited production version of their three-cylinder motorcycle for the US market. One of the most striking modifications was the three-pipe exhaust system and extended forks. With its 740cc engine, four-speed gearbox and a top speed of 170 km/h (106 mph), the Triumph Hurricane is a firm favourite with collectors.

**MEGA FACT**
*Fewer than 1,200 Hurricanes had been built when Triumph closed its factory in 1974. Despite this, the model made its mark and greatly influenced motorcycle design that followed.*

# INDIAN CHIEF

The Indian Chief dominated the motorcycle market for an incredible twenty years! But by the 1950s, the bike was outdated compared to its adversary, the Harley Knucklehead. Nearly 12,000 Chiefs were built in a choice of black, red, blue and white. Reaching a top speed of 137 km/h (85 mph), they weren't exactly the fastest bikes around, but with their smooth, classic looks – who cared!

# HONDA GOLD WING ASPENCADE, 1100cc SE

Launched in 1975, the original Honda GL™1000 Gold Wing was Japan's biggest, most complex bike ever produced. With a performance that matched anything on the market, the Gold Wing revolutionised motorcycle design. Then, in 1984, the Gold Wing Aspencade (shown right) was introduced. A new 1100cc engine and high-performance chassis were the basis of this luxury tourer. The hydraulic valve adjuster system provided quicker starts, faster warm-ups – and quieter running.

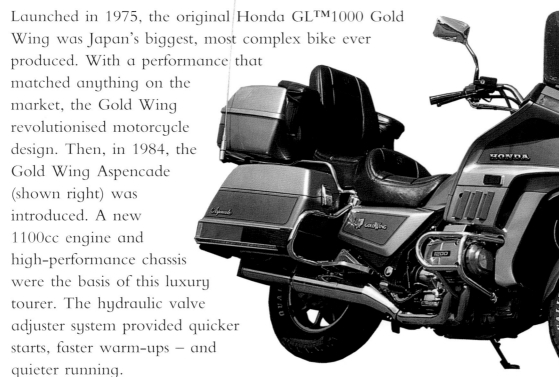

# ARIEL SQUARE FOUR

Production of the Ariel Square Four began in England in 1930. The design used two crankshafts geared together with the two vertical twin-cylinders arranged in a square formation (hence its name).

In 1949, the engine was redesigned with a light alloy block and head to form the Mark I. The Square Four Mark II came along in 1953, featuring detachable light alloy exhaust manifolds on each side.

# NORTON COMMANDO

The first Norton Commando motorcycle can be traced back to the late 1940s, when the Model 7 Twin was launched. This evolved into the 650cc Dominator and 750cc Atlas, before being launched as the 750cc Commando in 1967. During its 10 years in production, the Commando was very popular. In a pole conducted in the UK it was voted 'Machine of the Year' for five successive years (1968-1972). Enhanced by its light weight and slim profile, the 1969 chassis featured special engine mountings which helped to reduce vibration.

# BROUGH SUPERIOR SS100

The Rolls-Royce of motorcycles, Brough-Superior is surely the most distinguished marque in motorcycle history. Powerful and expensive, the SS100s were introduced in 1925 and are now one of the most sought-after of all collectors' bikes, not least because of their connection with English soldier and author, T.E. Lawrence (Lawrence of Arabia). Brough achieved many racing successes and speed records – in 1938 one bike reached 290 km/h (180 mph) in Budapest. Unfortunately the rider, Eric Fernihough, crashed and was killed on the return run, and his record was never officially recorded.

**MEGA FACT**
*Lawrence of Arabia (1888-1935) was an enthusiastic motorcyclist and owned many Brough motorcycles!*

# MATCHLESS G3L

Founded in 1899, Matchless was one of the first British motorcycle manufacturers. The 1941 G3L was a typical single-cylinder machine. Over 80,000 were built just for the British forces during World War II. Okay, so they're not the most elegant of machines, but the G3L was built for its sturdiness, reliability and endurance – not for its looks! This 347cc, 16.6 bhp machine, with a four-speed gearbox and a weight of 134 kg (295 lb), was one of the first British bikes to feature hydraulically damped telescopic forks.

**MEGA CLASSIC**
*G3Ls intended for desert use were painted a sandy colour as camouflage.*

# THE MONSTERS

Introducing the world's most powerful motorcycles ever made – the top speed of a Harley VR1000 is off the speedometer of most cars, let alone most motorcycles! Read on to find out more about these monster road bikes, including the difference between a sport bike, a trailbreaker and an ultra cycle!

## A TOP MONSTER

This Harley-Davidson VR1000 is a prime example of a powerful 'monster' bike. Its amazing engine has a pulling-power equal to the joint efforts of no less than 135 horses!

**MEGA FACT**
*Because of its power and manoeuvrability, US police are once again choosing the traditional Harley to patrol many city streets.*

**MEGA FACT**
*Most motorcycles have manual gearboxes. Only a few companies, like Honda and Moto Guzzi, have designed semi- and automatic models.*

# MONSTER BIKE MUST-HAVES

Mega powerful models have these common features:
- **A big muffler** to reduce the noise of the powerful engine
- A curved windshield, forcing the air smoothly over and around the motorcycle
- **Tapered styling** at the back to reduce wind-drag, therefore increasing speed
- High-performance tyres to give stability at top speeds

## FAST AND FURIOUS!

Japanese bikes may take the lead in many motorcycle sports today, but US Harleys are still tops on the dirt track.

## MEGA FACT
*In October 1970, Harley rider Cal Rayborn reached an amazing speed of 427 km/h (265.5 mph) on his cigar-shaped bike at the Salt Lake Flats in Utah, USA.*

# SUZUKI BANDIT

Top Japanese manufacturers Suzuki have a long history of producing high-performance machines like the Bandit pictured here. In 2000, this model received a complete makeover, giving it the agility of a middleweight sport bike and a top speed of 206 km/h (128 mph). This only improved upon the award-winning performance and style which have already made the Bandit a cult classic.

**MEGA FACT**
The most popular era for motorcycles to date was the late 1960s, when British makers alone built 70,000 bikes per year.

# TRIUMPH T509 SPEED TRIPLE

Tom Cruise made this striking motorcycle famous in his 2000 film, *Mission Impossible II*. Its stunning hi-tech appearance, combined with the awesome performance of a superbike, provided the attitude that's perfect for an action movie. Thanks to its extreme popularity, the Speed Triple has helped re-establish Triumph as one of the top marques in the industry.

**MEGA FAST**
The world's first eight-cylinder motorcycle was built by an American aviator and engine producer, Glenn Curtiss.

# ROKON TRAILBREAKER

The Rokon Trailbreaker was designed to go anywhere! This all-terrain motorcycle can climb steep mountain slopes, plough through the deepest mud, or haul heavy loads. It's popular with firefighters, farmers, mountaineers and hunters.

Trailbreakers have even been used by Brazilian Marines, who found the vehicles more capable in muddy terrain than some of their own tracked army vehicles.

# ULTRA AVENGER

Ultra cycles are custom-built bikes which are designed to suit each individual rider. Choosing from hundreds of options means you can create the bike of your dreams. It comes at a price though – US$25,000 for this 1999 Ultra Avenger!

# RALLY AND RACE

Motorcycle racing began around the same time as motorcar racing – in the late 1890s. And also like car racing, there are a number of different classes and categories. With events including Speedway, Rally, Grand Prix, Superbike, Enduro, Tourist Trophy (T.T.), Desert, American and Sidecar racing, there's something for everyone! Let's start with a look at Motocross and Superbike racing.

**MEGA FACT**
*Motocross riders must use the same motorcycle throughout a race, with repairs made between heats if necessary.*

*Motocross races are among the most challenging of events, with up to 40 riders competing on an open-terrain course.*

**MEGA FAST**
*Motocross races last only 40 minutes or less for each of two heats.*

*Spectacular jumps are part of the excitement of Motocross, so good suspension is critical for protecting the rider against bumps.*

*With a 249cc, liquid-cooled, single-cylinder two-stroke engine, and a revolutionary aluminium frame, the 2001 CR250R (above) is one of the world's most advanced 250 MX bikes.*

# SUPERBIKE RACING

First run in 1937, The Daytona 200 (it's a 200-mile race!) is America's most famous Superbike competition. These motorcycles must look like any ordinary model used on the road, but the Superbike rules limit four-cylinder bikes to 750cc, while two-cylinder machines are allowed to have a capacity of up to 1000cc. The tyres on Superbikes have no tread pattern. In dry weather, plain rubber (called a 'slick') gives the best grip. Wet weather tyres have a deep centre channel to drain away water.

## MX MADNESS
International Motocross courses must be 1.5 to 5 km (1 to 3 miles) long, with steep uphill as well as downhill grades, wet or muddy areas, and turns of varying difficulty.

## MX TERRAIN
Motocross bikes have special features to deal with their rough country courses. The engine and frame are set high to avoid rocks, and there are massive springs to ease the ride over bumps. Tyres are deep-cut and chunky to allow good grip on slippery or muddy surfaces.

**MEGA FACT**
*Motocross and other off-road tyres are called 'knobblies'.
Can you see why?*

# DRAG RACING

Drag racing takes place between two vehicles over a 400-metre (1/4 mile) straight track. The bikes vary from production models to huge twin-engined supercharged machines. Sprinting is the European variation of Drag, in which a single rider races against the clock. The dragster's secret of transmitting power to the track is having a very wide rear tyre, as on this 1977 Kawasaki 2400cc. It can reach a top speed of 300 km/h (186 mph).

# SPEEDWAY

Speedway is a form of dirt-track racing where stripped-down bikes race anti-clockwise on an oval track covered with cinders. Races are only four laps, so they're over very quickly. The 500cc Speedway motorcycles run on alcohol, have no gears and no brakes – just a kill switch! Riders have to slow down by sliding the back wheel of the machines through turns. The Kyokuto KT2 (right), which roughly translated means 'sunrise', is the most famous Japanese engine to have hit the Speedway track.

## THE T.T. RACES

The Tourist Trophy (or T.T.) is probably the best known and most demanding of all European motorcycle races. First run in 1907 on the Isle of Man, England, the T.T. attracted riders from all over Europe. But the natural obstacles of the road circuit made it extremely dangerous, and in 1977 it lost its status as a World Championship event. The race is run in various divisions determined by cycle size and racer experience. Sidecar races have also been held here.

# GRAND PRIX

At present, Grand Prix motorcycle races are those that apply to the World Championship of Drivers, although the term is also used to describe other, less prestigious events. The World Championships, made up of a series of Grand Prix races, began in 1949, but it took until the 1961 Argentine Grand Prix for the first event to be held outside Europe. Although there are World Championship classes for 125 and 250 solos, the 500cc is still considered the premier Grand Prix class.

**MEGA FACT**
*Ice racing is popular in Scandinavia and Eastern Europe. The tracks are usually circular, so fierce-looking spiked tyres are used to grip the ice. Riders protect their knees and elbows by padding them with lengths of old tyre.*

**MEGA RACERS**
*The latest computerised data-recording equipment monitors a bike's performance as it speeds around the Grand Prix circuit.*

# AMAZING BUT TRUE

# EVEL KNIEVEL

Born on 17 October 1938, in Montana, USA, Robert Craig Knievel – or Evel Knievel as he became better known – is probably the most famous motorcycle stunt rider of all time!

An outstanding skier and ice hockey player, he began his daredevil career in 1965. Forming a troupe called Evel Knievel's Motorcycle Daredevils, he regularly rode through fire walls and was towed at 320 km/h (200 mph) behind dragster race cars while holding on to a parachute!

In 1966, Evel decided to start touring alone. On 1 January 1968, he jumped 45 metres (151 feet) across the fountains in front of Caesar's Palace in Las Vegas, USA. Although he cleared the fountains, his landing was a complete disaster, and his injuries left him in a coma for 30 days. The injuries didn't stop him though, and Evel continued performing his daredevil stunts around the world until his retirement in 1976.

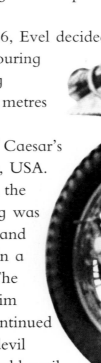

# EVEL'S MEMORABLE MOMENTS:

1968    On New Year's Day, Evel crashed while jumping the fountains at Caesar's Palace in Las Vegas, USA.

1970    Successfully cleared 13 cars in Seattle, USA, on 9 September.

1971    Set a world record in Ontario, Canada, by jumping 19 Dodge cars.

1974    Successfully jumped 40.5 metres (135 feet) over three trucks at the Canadian National Exposition on 20 August.

1975    Over 90,000 spectators at Wembley Stadium, London, watched as Evel crashed upon landing, breaking his pelvis after clearing 13 double-decker buses.

1976    Evel suffered a concussion and two broken arms during an attempt to jump a tank full of live sharks in Chicago, USA. For the first time a bystander was also injured, eventually losing an eye. Evel decided to retire from major performances.

# ⊙ RECORD-BREAKERS ⊙

⊙ The world's tallest rideable motorcycle (left) was built by Tom Wiberg of Sweden. This record-breaking vehicle measures an amazing 2.3 metres (7.5 ft) high and 4.7 metres (15 ft) long!

⊙ The Harley-Davidson Owners Group (HOG) is the world's largest company-sponsored motorcycle enthusiasts' group – with over 400,000 members in more than 1,000 branches world-wide.

⊙ The fastest time for a run over 400 metres (440 yds) is 6.19 seconds, held by American Tony Lang (above), who rode a supercharged Suzuki in Gainesville, Florida, USA, in 1994.

⊙ In 1996, Douglas and Roger Bell, from Western Australia, designed and built a bike (above) with a record length of 7.6 metres (25 ft).

⊙ The world's most expensive production motorcycle, the Morbidelli 850 V8 (left), sold for a great US$98,400 (approx. £56,700), in 1998!

These are the machines that make heads turn! They may not be the sleekest or fastest vehicles ever built, but these motorcycles and scooters are certainly among the most interesting. Let's start with a look at the super long Bohmerland!

### THREE'S A CROWD!

This 1928 Bohmerland from the Czech Republic was an extra-long motorcycle that seated three people. Many features combined to make this bike a real oddball. Apart from its great length, it had two fuel tanks which were mounted on each side of the rear wheel (rather than under the engine as usual) and the frame was made of tubular steel.

*Unfortunately, the Bohmerland was not produced in great numbers due to the start of World War II, in 1939.*

# MEGA GOLF CART

The Bobcat was the ultimate caddy, enabling golfers to speed round the course in record time. Little is known about this unusual vehicle, but we do know that this two-wheeled linkster had a clever self-standing centre stand, which was activated when the golfer's weight left the seat. Although the cart is no longer in production, the Chicago-based manufacturer is still in business, building Bobcat skip loaders.

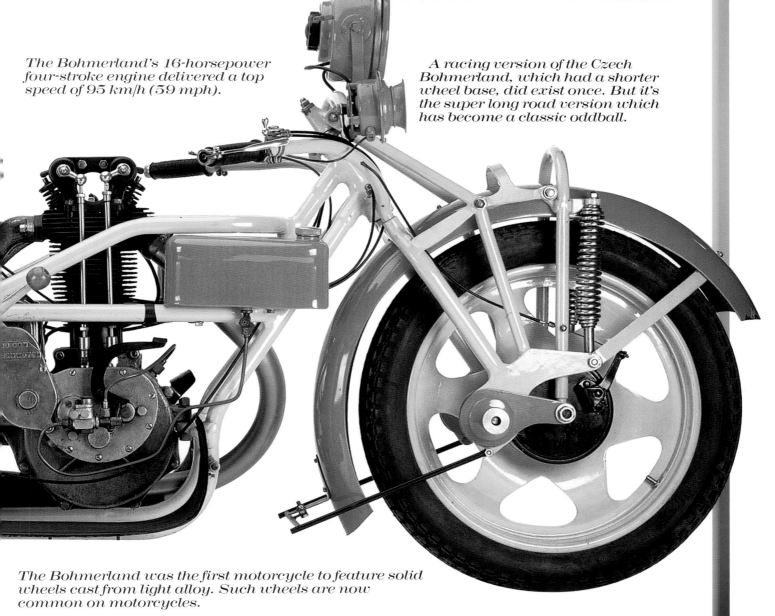

*The Bohmerland's 16-horsepower four-stroke engine delivered a top speed of 95 km/h (59 mph).*

*A racing version of the Czech Bohmerland, which had a shorter wheel base, did exist once. But it's the super long road version which has become a classic oddball.*

*The Bohmerland was the first motorcycle to feature solid wheels cast from light alloy. Such wheels are now common on motorcycles.*

# AUTOPED

The Autoped was little more than a motorised version of a child's scooter. Made in New York City in 1917, this model was an instant success as it allowed riders to weave in and out of the confused mixture of trolleys, horses and cars that crowded the city's streets at the time.

*The Autoped's steering column could be folded down for easy storage.*

*The seatless Autoped was designed to be driven standing up!*

# THE WILLIAMS

Although it never went into full production, the 1917 Williams is one of the most unusual motorcycles ever made. Note the footboards – they're also a mechanism which the rider pumps to start the engine. The 3-cylinder engine was built into the rear of the machine, and it would spin with the rear wheel.

# CUSHMAN MODEL 52

After World War II, the Cushman company took advantage of the scooter boom in the USA and manufactured a range of models, including the 52 (below). This stylish scooter boasted a 4-horsepower engine delivering a top speed of 65 km/h (40 mph). The Model 52 was nicknamed the 'Turtleback'. Can you see why?

**MEGA FACT**
*Scooters are becoming fashionable again with the help of recent cool models like the plastic-bodied Yamaha BW12.*

# NER-A-CAR

The 1923 'Nearly-A-Car' was truly an oddball! The maker's choice of name was meant to convince customers that the machine combined the best qualities of both a car and a motorcycle. It was more enclosed than most motorcycles, with lots of mudguarding to prevent the rider's clothes from getting dirty. Its low centre of gravity also made for easier handling.

**MEGA FACT**
*The Ner-A-Car is said to have been especially popular with vicars because the open frame enabled them to ride wearing their cassocks!*

# GLOSSARY

**AERODYNAMICS** The science of shaping machines to slip easily through the air. Smooth, slim shapes are better than boxy shapes.

**BHP** Brake Horse Power, a measurement of the engine's maximum power output.

**CARBURETTOR** An instrument for mixing fuel and air into a combustible vapour.

**CRADLE** Motorcycle frame which places the engine between two frame tubes.

**DISC BRAKE** A brake which has two pads that grip either side of a metal disc.

**EXHAUST**
The part of an engine through which wasted gases or steam pass. It ends with a silencing unit, which reduces noise.

FAIRING  A front enclosure to improve the motorcycle's aerodynamics, or the rider's comfort.

GIRDER FORKS  A common form of front suspension on early machines. The front wheel is held in a set of forks which are attached to the steering head by parallel links.

IGNITION TIMING  An electrical system that produces a spark to ignite the fuel/air mixture in a petrol engine.

MEGAPHONE  A tapered performance exhaust.

PLUNGER  Rear suspension system where the axle is mounted between two vertical springs.

RPM  Revolutions Per Minute, a unit of measure used to express the rotational speed of an engine.

SUPERCHARGER  Device for compressing the engine's incoming charge.

THROTTLE  Device that controls the quantity of fuel or fuel/air mixture entering an engine.

TORQUE  The maximum amount of force produced at a specific speed.

UNIT CONSTRUCTION  The construction of the engine and gearbox within the same casings.

V-TWIN  An engine layout in which the cylinders are placed in a 'V' formation.

PRE-UNIT  Engine and gearbox constructed in separate units, common on older machines.

**MEGA CLASSIC**
*The 1958 Harley Davidson FLH Duo-Glide (shown here) is a super stylish classic. The Duo-Glide emblem on the front fender distinguishes the '58 from earlier models.*

# INDEX

# Picture Credits

T=top; B=bottom; C=centre
13 EMAP Motoring Picture Library; 20 Ian Kerr; 21 Alvey & Towers; 22T Garry
Stuart; 22B Empics Sports Photo Agency; 23T Ian Kerr; 23B Alvey & Towers; 24 PA
Photos; 25T PA Photos; 25CL Tom Wiberg; 25CR Tony Lang; 25BL Garry Stuart

All other pictures Alligator Books Limited.